Bear's
Curiosity Book

A QUARTO BOOK

First published in the UK in 1994 by
New Burlington Press

ISBN 1853 48 643 4

This book was produced by
Quarto Children's Books Ltd.
The Fitzpatrick Building
188–194 York Way
London N7 9QP

Art Director: Louise Jervis
Managing Editor: Christine Hatt
Designer: Dawn Apperley

Manufactured in Singapore by Bright Arts Pte. Ltd.
Printed in Singapore by Star Standard Industries Pte. Ltd.

Bear's
Curiosity Book

WRITTEN BY

DAVID HOWGRAVE-GRAHAM

ILLUSTRATED BY

SIMONE ABEL

NEW
BURLINGTON
BOOKS

Contents

6   Bear's busy day

8   Who's been here?

10   A hide-and-seek alphabet

12   What's wrong here?

14   Help Bear count

16   Big and little things

18   Spot the shape

20   Mud tale

22   Opposites

24   Amazing animal facts

26   What's heavy?

28   Apples from apples

30   Colour mix-up

32   Bear about town

34   Ways of sorting

36 Water wizardry

38 Bear's pattern play

40 Air riddle

42 A Bear for all seasons

44 Out shopping

46 Body bits and Bear care

48 Moving is confusing

50 What are things made of?

52 Sticky stuff

54 Bears at work

56 Food for thought

58 Stone story

60 Moods Bear feels

62 Just looking around

Bear's busy day

Bear doesn't measure time. He enjoys it. We use clocks and watches to measure time. We have words to describe time passing - minutes make hours make days make years.

When Bear finishes this page, more time will have passed. Try to spot the mouse in every picture.

 It is 8 o'clock. Bear's alarm clock wakes him up. He has a busy day ahead.

"A clean bear is a healthy bear," thinks Bear.

 Bear likes to dress, but he does make a mess.

 It is 9 o'clock. Time for breakfast. Soldiers and eggs are what Bear likes best.

 By 10 o'clock Bear is at school. Bear likes to paint. Bear's friends just wish he wouldn't paint them, too.

 It is 1 o'clock. Bear is hungry. It is time for a picnic in the park.

 "Shopping is fun," thinks Bear. He likes to help, but sometimes things go wrong!

 It is 4 o'clock and time for a party. Friends come and there is food and fun for everyone.

 Bear likes a bath before bed. There is still some time to play.

 By 7 o'clock Bear is in bed. Today was a busy day. Bear will sleep well. Tomorrow will be another busy day.

Who's been here?

Can you help Bear match the
tracks to whatever made them?

Match the right shoes to the
right person.

A hide-and-seek alphabet

How many alphabears can you spot?

Aa astronaut

Bb boat

Cc clown

Dd dinosaur

Ii insect

Jj juggler

Kk kangaroo

Ll lion

Mm monster

Rr robot

Ss snowbear

Tt train

Uu umbrella

Vv volcano

Ee elephant   **Ff** fireworks   **Gg** gorilla   **Hh** helicopter

Nn nose   **Oo** octopus   **Pp** pirate   **Qq** queen

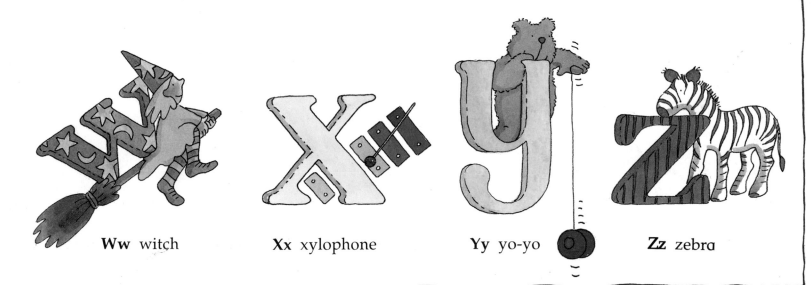

Ww witch   **Xx** xylophone   **Yy** yo-yo   **Zz** zebra

What's wrong here?

BABY GOES IN BUGGY   CAMEL LIVES IN DESERT   WHALE LIVES IN OCEAN   PENGUIN LIVES ON ICEBERG   FROG LIVES ON LILY PAD   KOALA LIVES IN TREE   PIG LIVES IN STY

To sort this out, Bear has to cheat. You might find it easier just to turn the book upside down.

MOUSE LIVES IN MOUSE HOLE   FISH LIVES IN FISH BOWL   BABY EATS ICE CREAM   DOG EATS BONE   SPIDER MAKES WEB   BIRD MAKES NEST   KANGAROO GOES IN POUCH

13

Help Bear count

When it comes to counting, Bear is a nitwit. Some of Bear's friends have got together to make it simpler for him.

There is only **one** Curiosity Bear.

Two long crocodiles

Three woolly sheep

Four feathery geese

Five baby elephants

6   **Six** tall giraffes

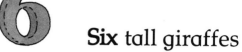 **7**   **Seven** fluffy rabbits

8   **Eight** waddling ducks

9   **Nine** naughty mice

10   **Ten** love birds on a branch

 0   The problem is, Bear will remember nothing. This is the symbol for nothing.

Big and little things

A flea is so little that Bear needs a magnifying glass to see it. Fleas bite, so this flea is no friend of Bear. But Bear does have friends of all shapes and sizes.

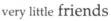

very little **friends**

little friends

big friends

bigger friends

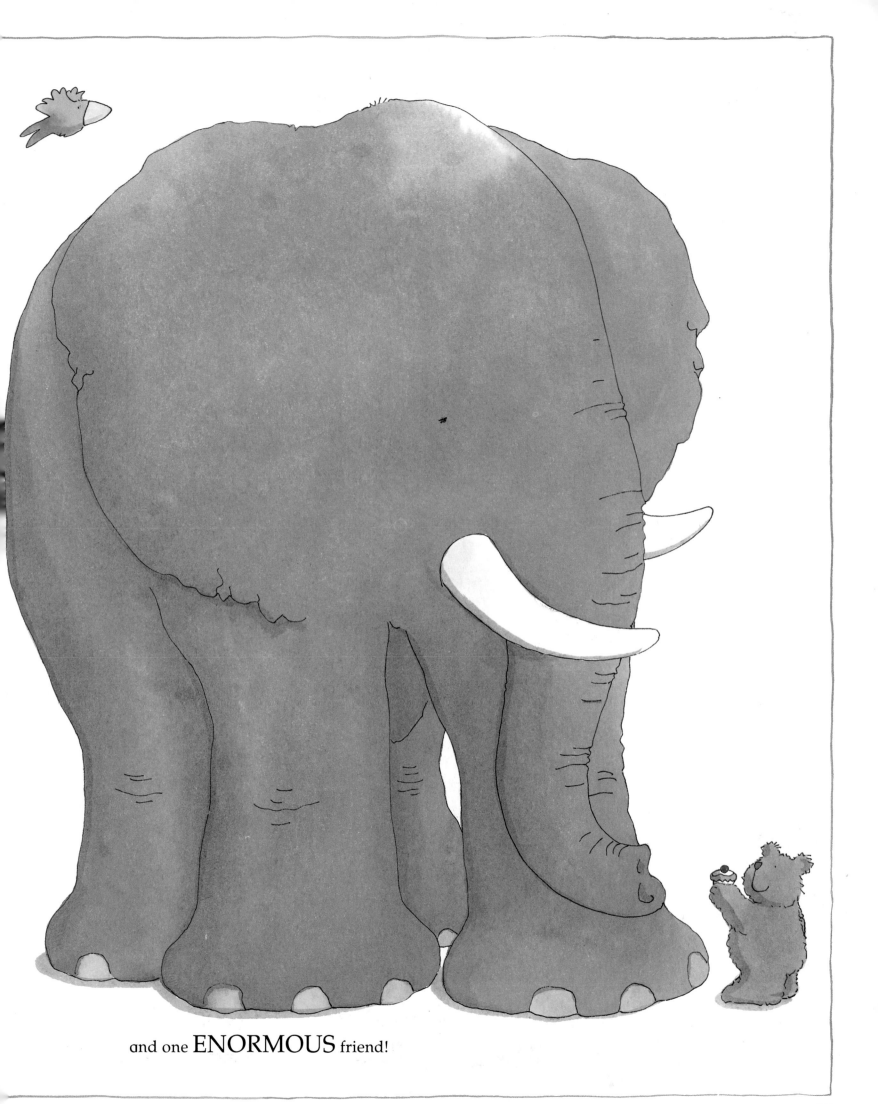

and one ENORMOUS friend!

Spot the shape

This plate is a **circle**.  This book is a

 **rectangle**. This piece of cake is a **triangle**.

This biscuit  is **square**. This egg is **oval**.  Bear's kite is

 **diamond**-shaped. This starfish is shaped like a **star**.

Bear draws a house.

 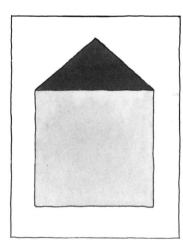 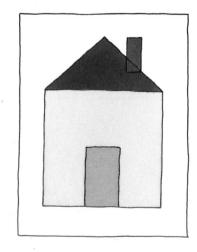

Bear starts
with a **square**.

He adds a **triangle**
for the roof . . .

. . . and **rectangles** for the
door and chimney.

Sandwich shapes

One square
sandwich . . .

. . . cut like this . . .

. . . gives you
two triangles.

Put the two triangles
like this for a diamond.

Cut the sandwich
like this . . .

. . . and you have
two rectangles.

Cut the rectangles
like this . . .

. . . and you have
four squares.

The wheels on Bear's
bike are circles. He
wouldn't go far if
they were squares!

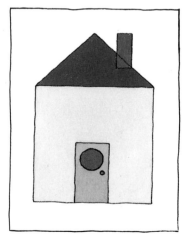

Then he adds **circles**
for the door window,
and for the door knob.

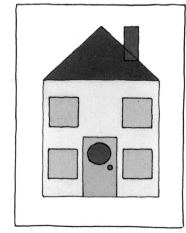

Then he adds four
squares for the
windows.

"How many **squares**
are there now?"
wonders Bear.

Mud tale

Bear calls this mud.
We also call it soil.

Sometimes it is hard and dry. Bear doesn't find it easy to dig.

When mud is wet it gets everywhere!

Look at some soil. What do you see?

Lots of animals live in soil.

There are also bits of rock, roots, leaves, dead plants, and animals.

Grass, flowers, vegetables, bushes, and trees all need its goodness to grow.

tree

leaves

roots

worm

woodlouse

Plants need mud.

If you put mud in a pot and sow a seed in it, you can grow your own plant.

Your plant needs light and water, too. Keep it by a window. Water it often.

People make pots out of a special kind of mud called clay. Some people also make their homes out of mud.

For Sale

Animals make their homes in mud. Swallows, rabbits, moles, badgers . . . and even bears!

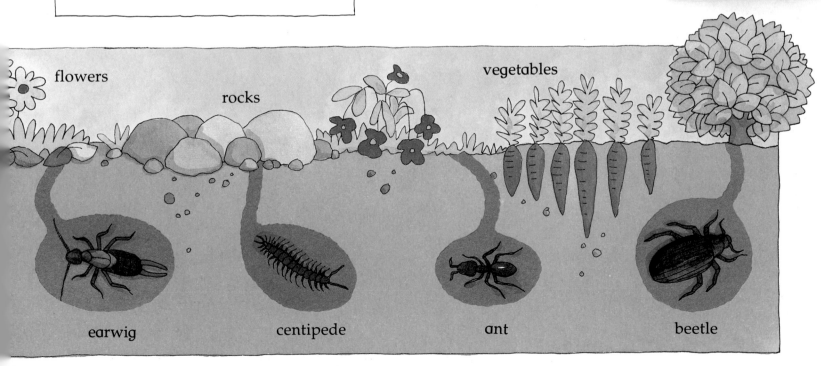

flowers

rocks

vegetables

earwig

centipede

ant

beetle

Opposites

white bird

black bird

The end of the next page is the opposite of the beginning of this page.

Bear is **awake**.
It is **light**.

up

down

BIG elephant

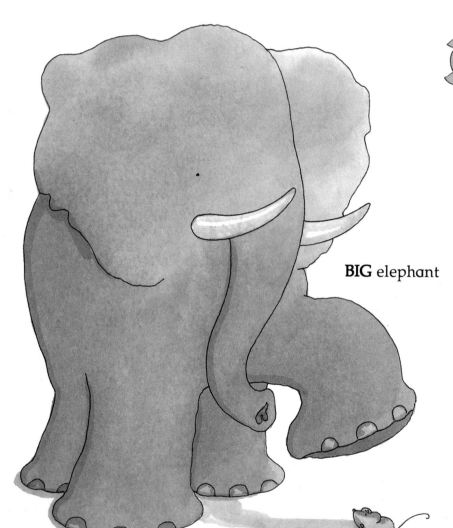

little mouse

"Boy, are you short," says the **long** snake to the **short** worm.

open

Which are the opposites here?

The bucket is **full**.

Mouse is **dry**.

The bucket is **empty**.

Mouse is **wet**.

over

under

shut

Problems with doors

in door

out door

high head

low door

narrow door

wide hippo

Bear is **asleep**.

It is **dark**.

23

Amazing animal facts

Bear can't think what to do with these facts, but he would like to share them with you. Maybe you'll need to know them some day... but maybe you won't... and perhaps you'll just forget.

Slowest animal
3–toed sloth

Longest insect
Stick insect

Longest snake
Python

Noisiest animal
Howling monkey

Most legs
A millipede has 750 legs.

Longest sleeper
The barrow squirrel
sleeps for 9 months a year.

Biggest nest
American bald eagle

Longest horns
Indian water buffalo

Largest egg
Ostrich

Fastest land animal
Cheetah

What's heavy?

Bear's apples are both the same weight. Weight is a measuring word.

As Bear grows, he will weigh more. He will grow heavier. Bear will never measure weight, but can you think why you might?

Which of Bear's cases is so heavy that he can't lift it?

Who is heavier, elephant or mouse?

These balloons are light!

This bucket is middling heavy.

These weights are very heavy.

Please help Bear sort out which of these are heavy and which are light.

Apples from apples

Bear bites into an apple.
"What are these black things
in the middle?" he wonders.

The black things are seeds.
These will make new trees.

A seed grows
in the ground.

Rain helps the
seed to grow.

It also needs light
from the sun.

Food from the soil
helps it to grow some more.

After a few years it will
grow into a small tree.

One spring the
tree will blossom.

As the blossom
fades, apples will form.

By the autumn, the apples
will be big and ready to eat.

Bears grow too.

Once Bear was
little like this.

Now he is sort
of middly.

This is Dad. One day Bear
will be as big as Dad.

Colour mix–up

Rainbows happen when light shines through rain. You cannot reach one, but you can see all the colours in it. What are they?

These objects are sorted by colour. What other things do you think of when you see these colours?

Bear has painted a pretty picture, but it is wrong! Perhaps you could tell him what colours he should have used?

Look what happens when colours mix.

Bear about town

Everything in the border can be spotted in the town Bear would like your help to find them all.

ferry

bicycle

motorbike

car

ambulance

police car

train

bus

lorry

rubbish cart

car park

fountain

aeroplane

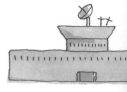
control tower

motor boat

dinghy

tug boat

tanker

church

petrol station

factory

skyscraper

aeroplane hangar

bridge

Football Bear

Ways of sorting

Bear has lots of counters.
"How many different ways
can I sort them?" wonders Bear.

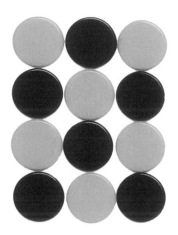

small only

big only

Bear is very messy. Can you
help him sort out his room?

small yellow

big yellow

all yellow

all red

small red

big red

Water wizardry

Bear often sees water.

He sees water
when he drinks it.

When water falls from clouds
he calls it rain. Rain collects in
rivers which flow to the sea.

At the sea Bear sees lots of
water. He doesn't know that
water covers most of the world.

Sometimes Bear doesn't see water that is there.

Bear's snowman is made
of water that has frozen.

When heat from the sun
melts it, Bear sees a puddle.

Later, even the puddle has
gone. What happened?

Water works

Bear's rubber duck
floats on water . . .

. . . but his soap sinks.

When Bear turns
on the tap, water
flows down . . .
"Why down?"
he wonders.

Water is always level . . .   . . . even when tipped in a jug.

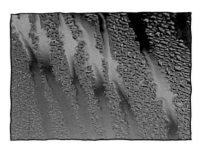

When Bear has a shower
the window steams up.

On the cold window the
steam turns back to water.

Look at the pretty frost
patterns water makes
when it is very cold.

"How do boats float on it?"
wonders Bear. "I don't."

Trees, plants, animals, and
people all need water to live.

What we eat is made mostly
of water . . . so are we!

His empty cup floats . . .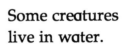

. . . but when it is full of
water, it doesn't.

But he c_ _ _quirt water
from a s_ _ _ _ _ _ _ _

. . . like a fountain.

**Some creatures
live in water.**

Fish and whales do.
What else can you
think of?

37

Bear's pattern play

Patterns are everywhere. We see them at home. We see them in nature. In a pattern Bear sees the same shape many times.

Lots of things have patterns.

Can you help Bear to find the hat, scarf and gloves to match his sweater?

The squares on Bear's draughts board make a pattern.

The draughts can also make a pattern.

These are the same draughts, but the pattern has gone.

Look at these patterns. Try making some of your own.

Bear has folded a
piece of paper like
a concertina.

He cuts the folded
paper into the shape
of a bear.

Bear has made a
pattern of bears.

Air riddle

Bear's glass is empty...
well, it looks empty.
Actually it is full of
air. We cannot see the
air, so we say the glass is empty.
Air is all around us.

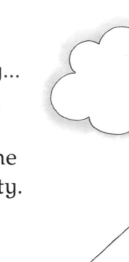

"I can see things that fly
in the air," thinks Bear,
"but I cannot see the air."

When Bear blows
up his balloon, he
fills it with air.

When Bear blows
bubbles in his drink,
he sees the air.

When Bear breathes
in, he sucks in air.

When Bear breathes
out, he blows out air.

Which is heavier, air or water?
Bear's water wings are filled with air. They help him to float in his swimming pool.
Can you answer the question now?

But mostly Bear doesn't think about air.

When the air is cold we feel it.

When the air is hot we feel it.

Wind is moving air. When the wind blows we feel it.

A Bear for all seasons

Spring Bear

Summer Bear

Autumn Bear

Winter Bear

Out shopping

Bear has an empty basket and a full shopping list. What will Bear buy where? Can you help him?

One thing on Bear's list can't be found in any of these shops. What is it?

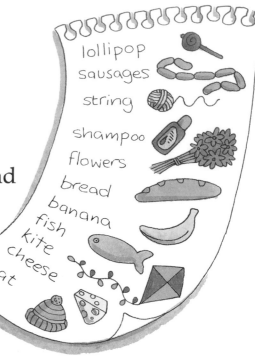

lollipop
sausages
string
shampoo
flowers
bread
banana
fish
kite
cheese
hat

Delicatessen

Bert's Bakery

Veg-ta-bear

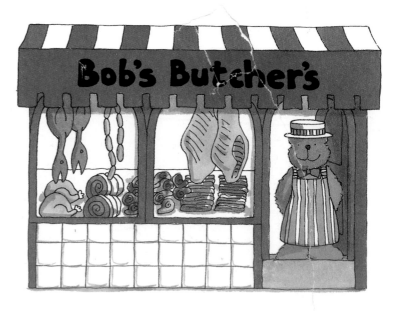

Bob's Butcher's

Ted's Toys

Lola's Sweet Shop

Fred's Fish

Horace's Hardware

Ready-to-wear-bear

Body bits and Bear care

In this touchy-feely and so on story
Bear uses many of his body bits.

"Country air will clear
my **head**," thinks Bear.

Bear's **ears** hear the buzz of
the bees. "Honey," thinks Bear.

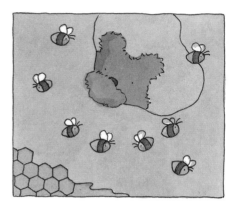

Bear's **eyes** follow the
bees to their nest.

Bear's **nose** smells
the honey.

He touches the
honey with his **paw**.

He tastes the honey
with his **tongue**.

Some bees sting Bear.
He feels the pain
through his **skin**.

His **legs** carry him away
as fast as he can run. His
arms beat off the bees . . .

. . . but his **tummy** is full
and his **legs** are tired, so
he sits on his **bottom**.

"Body bits have their uses," thinks Bear,
"but the next time I'll get my honey from a jar."

Bear brushes his teeth because he needs them to eat with. Teeth rot if they are not looked after.

Bear brushes his hair to keep it healthy and shiny.

Bear likes to keep himself clean. Dirty bears don't smell nice.

Bear exercises to keep his body in good shape. "A healthy bear is a beautiful bear," he thinks.

"Bodies aren't perfect," thinks Bear. "How do I scratch my back?"

Moving is confusing

Moving is a
funny business.

Some creatures fly . . .   like butterflies . . .   and bees . . .

**Others stick
to the ground.**

Bear uses two legs . . .   so do people . . .   except babies. They crawl . . .

  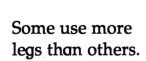

**Some use more
legs than others.**

Sometimes Bear uses four legs . . . like a dog.   Insects have six legs.

**People have invented
things to make
moving easier.**

Wheels and leg
power work well . . .

. . . with an engine
it's easier still.

Cars are more
comfortable.

and birds.

Things fall down
Bear doesn't know why.
He just knows that things fall down
. . . they don't fall up.

Bear is holding   If he lets go
a ball.   it drops.

If he throws it up in the
air it still comes down.

. . . rather like snakes slither.   Kangaroos hop.

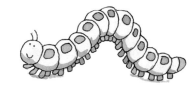

Spiders have eight legs.   Caterpillars have lots of legs.

Add wings to the engine
if you want to fly.

A crane is needed
to move this block.
To move anything up or
along needs effort . . .
"or a machine," thinks Bear.

What are things made of?

Bear is not reading this book. Bears can't read. And Bear doesn't know that his book was made from a tree.

Bear doesn't know what these things are made of. Do you?

Look at the first picture. Then help Bear to find what is missing from the other three.

WOOD

Wood comes from trees.

We use it in many ways. We can turn it into paper.

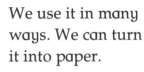

We burn it to keep warm.

We carve things out of it.

Bear's kitchen

Bear's kitchen without wood

50

METAL

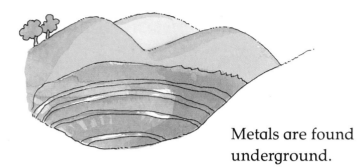

Metals are found underground.

Often they are mixed with rocks.

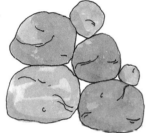

We melt metals to shape them. They are strong, and good for cutting things.

PLASTIC

Plastic is made from oil. Oil is found underground and under the oceans, like metals. It is made of animals and plants that died long, long ago.

Plastic can be made into any shape.

Bear's kitchen without metal

Bear's kitchen without plastic

Bears at work

Machines make work easier. How are these machines helping the busy bears?

all-terrain vehicle
(ATV)

dump truck

tractor and plough

digger

fork-lift tractor

mobile crane

combine harvester

bulldozer

trailer

tractor

cement mixer

"I'm glad there aren't any other pages about work in this book!" thinks Bear.

Food for thought

"I know bees make honey," thinks Bear, "but where do other foods come from?"

Match the photos to the pictures.

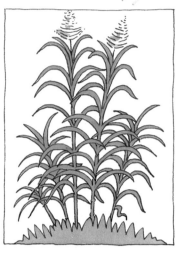

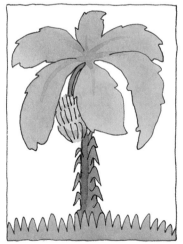

56

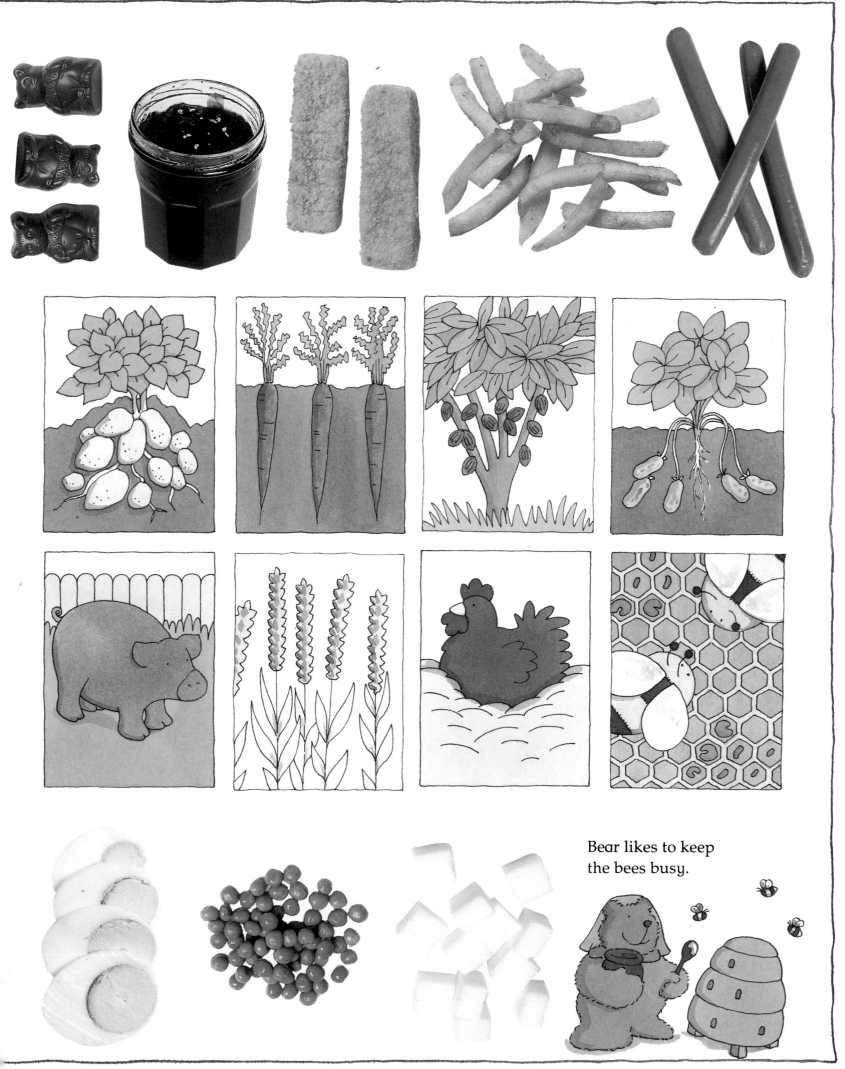

Bear likes to keep
the bees busy.

Stone story

Bear is holding a stone. It is just an ordinary little stone. Stones are everywhere. "Where do stones come from?" wonders Bear.

Mountains are made of stone.

Rain and wind break stones off the mountains.

Rivers carry them downhill . . .

. . . and over waterfalls . . .

. . . and far away. On their journey,

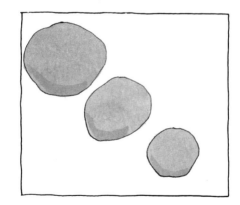

big stones break into smaller stones.

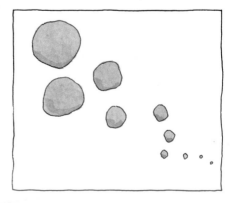

As years pass, small stones get smaller and smaller.

Some stones are even carried to the sea.

58

Bear's new house

This hole is where Bear's new house will be. The truck is filling the hole with **concrete**. **Concrete** is made mostly of **stone** and **sand**.

When it is hard **concrete** is very strong. The **stone** walls of Bear's house are also very strong. The window panes are made of **glass**.

Glass is made mostly of **sand**. **Sand** is made of tiny bits of **stone**. "It's a funny world," thinks Bear.

Bear is building a sandcastle. It is a very fine sandcastle . . .

. . . but Bear doesn't know that it is really a stone castle.

Sand is made of stones that are much littler than Bear's.

Moods Bear feels

Some feelings are good. Bear feels **kind**

when he does something for someone. He feels **friendly** when

he cuddles Mum. He feels **happy** when he gets what he wants.

Some feelings are bad. When Bear is **lazy**,

he doesn't want to do things. He feels **angry** when he doesn't

get his way. When he won't share his toys, he is **mean**.

Some feelings are just confusing. Bear feels **silly** when

his friends laugh at him. He feels **lonely** when

his friends don't play with him. He feels **sad**

when he has to say goodbye to a friend.

Feelings change. Funny thing – when Bear is **happy**

his friends seem to be **happy**.

Just looking around

Bear isn't always busy. Sometimes he stops to think. Bear is curious because the world is curious . . . and wherever he looks, Bear finds questions.

"How do you do that?"

"What do you want to be when you grow up?"

"Is anyone home?"

"What are you doing under this stone?"

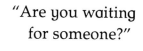

"Are you waiting for someone?"

"Where does the water go?"

"Where did you come from? Look what you've done to my lawn!"

"Will you come back tomorrow?"

"Can you make me a sweater for
my birthday?"

"Is there a pot of gold at
the end of the rainbow?"

"Where do you all go
in the daytime?"

"If I just keep walking, will I
get to the end of the world?"

"Life is full of questions.
How come some of the
answers are so hard?"